# Journaling Through The Dimensions Of Love

*All for The Sake of Love*

# Journaling Through The Dimensions Of Love

*All for The Sake of Love*

**Asha Cannon**

Journaling Through The Dimensions of Love

© 2020 by Asha Cannon

Living Water Books
Christian Division of Butterfly Typeface Publishing House,
Little Rock, Arkansas 72201

ISBN 978-1-7357073-9-6

All rights reserved. This book is protected by the copyright laws of the United States of America. This book may not be copied or reprinted for commercial gain or profit. Any portion thereof may not be reproduced or used in any manner whatsoever without the express written permission of Asha Cannon except for brief quotations in a book review or occasional page copying for personal or group study and encouraged.

Unless otherwise notes, all scripture quotations are from the King James Version Bible® Copyright ©1982 Used by permission

Scripture quotations marked Message (MSG) are from The Holy Bible, Message Version, Copyright © 1993. Used by Permission. All Rights Reserved

Unless otherwise notes, all scripture quotations are from the Amplified Version Bible® Copyright ©2015 Used by permission. All rights reserved

Unless otherwise notes, all scripture quotations are from the New International Version Bible® Copyright ©2011 Used by permission. All Rights reserved worldwide

Unless otherwise notes, all scripture quotations are from the New American Standard Bible ® Copyright ©2014 Used by permission. All Rights reserved worldwide

## A Tribute To Mother

The saying is, give people their roses while they are living.
Mom, you are planted deep in my heart. I look at you, and I see myself.
I see a gentle strength. I see a heart that loves so hard it hurts sometimes.
I see the woman I'd love to be because there's a true overcomer in you.
I see a smile and a confident sway in your dainty walk with every year you age. I pray I make you smile more than I make you cry.

Lord knows you have cried enough, but I see that God has blessed your latter days. I know some days are not perfect, yet you are truly perfect to me!
I love you, and always want you to be proud of me.
I thank you for being my #1 fan! I remember how you were at every grand opening, every speech, almost every ministering event that was close enough for you to attend! I hope this dedication plants another seed of love in your heart that goes deep to uproot any pains that you experienced from unfortunate events in your life! Thank you for your simplicity at times and Your grandness at others! I love you, twin!

Sincerely,

Your daughter, Asha

# A Tribute To Husband

*Dear Eric Cannon, on our 1st Valentine's Day,*

*you purchased this journal for me*

*titled, All For Love. I knew this journal had to be a journal*

*where the transformation I desired would soon come forth.*

*My heart desires to become a loving wife to the man who has loved me unconditionally. Our journey has not been a textbook perfect story; however, God has been the author of our love story from the moment we became more than friends! Thank you for never judging me, for thinking the world of me, and always desiring to be more like Christ.*

*I fell in love with you because you reflect a familiar person in my life that loves me beyond my flaws, which is Jesus Christ himself.*
*This season has just begun but redemption to love through marriage has never been more satisfying, fulfilling, and worth it!*
*In your words, "I love you like Jesus loves you!"*

Sincerely,

Your Loving Wife, Asha

# TABLE OF CONTENTS

A Tribute To Mother ............................................................ 7
A Tribute To Husband........................................................... 8
Preface ................................................................................ 11
Bankrupt Without Love ...................................................... 14

### Chapter One
The Call To Love ................................................................ 17

### Chapter Two
Past Perfections Brought Future Blemishes ................... 25

### Chapter Three
God Unmasked His Fears ................................................. 41

### Chapter Four
God Uncovered Her Scars ................................................ 49

### Chapter Five
The Power Of Prayer......................................................... 55
   Blended Family Prayer................................................. 59

## Chapter Six
I Can't Bake This Up...................................................... 67

## Chapter Seven
You Can Only Play One Position ...................................... 73

## Chapter Eight
Love Isn't Enough ............................................................ 83

## Chapter Nine
Love the Hell Out Of Them.............................................. 91
Prayer of Acceptance....................................................... 93
Welcome to The Family....................................................94
Conclusion........................................................................95
The Publisher...................................................................99

# Preface

During my alone time, The Lord told me to write out our love story. The onset of our love journey came from my husband and me, desiring to become closer to God and love one another in a way that neither of us experienced in previous relationships. Sharing our story highlighted my Overall view of love and my perception of God's love for me. God wants us to see that every relationship surrounding us reflects our heart. As you travel through the pages of our love story, you will find various details of our lives that either affected our growth or brought forth fulfillment. I learned that God's will for an assignment is never just about the individual, marriage, or children. It is all about whom he has planted in our lives.

The purpose of *Journaling Through The Dimensions Of Love* was to bring us into full view of God's great love. God presented questions to us that we now share with you.

*Take a brief pause here*

Now ask yourself,

- How do I relate to love?
- How does my heart encounter love?
- How do I perceive love?
- What is my motive (reason) for loving those in my life?
- What is my commitment to love?

Then lastly, as Christians,

- How can we love the way Christ loved?

When situations and circumstances attempt to shove us into this bubble, causing us to make fearful decisions, we invite only those we think won't hurt us. As I vulnerably share with you how God has enlarged my capacity to view love differently, I challenge you to understand the term love. I pray that you recognize God is Love. I have discovered that in the name of love, many things become misconstrued. The power of God's love is often minimized to our understanding and experiences, thus causing us to create a distorted view of love that ultimately hinders progress in God and fulfilling his will for our life. I am not perfect, nor do I consider myself a master of love coach, but

I have discovered an all-consuming reckless love of God in my quest for love! The love of God has transformed my life in such a way that it allows me to love uninhibitedly! God's love can dismantle any blockade the enemy establishes. When love is applied in the difficult moments, God becomes immense in the lives of those that need to see and feel Him most!

The Bible asks,

> *If you love those who love you, what reward will you get? Are not even the tax collectors doing that? And if you greet only your people, what are you doing more than others? Do not even pagans do that? Be perfect; therefore, as your Heavenly Father is perfect. – Matthew 5:46-48.*

Let this book challenge you to allow God to take you through different dimensions and levels of love for Him. Watch how love comes in like a flood to eradicate any wrong concepts of itself and pour into you a fresh new overflow of Him. I assure you, your cup will overflow, and relationships in every facet around you shall be transformed for God's Glory!

## Bankrupt Without Love

*If I speak with human eloquence and angelic ecstasy but do not love, I'm nothing but the creaking of a rusty gate.*

*² If I speak God's word with power, revealing all his mysteries and making everything plain as day, and if I have faith that says to a mountain, "Jump," and it jumps, but I don't love, I'm nothing.*

*³⁻⁷ If I give everything I own to the poor and even go to the stake to be burned as a martyr, but I do not love, I've gotten nowhere. So, no matter what I say, what I believe, and what I do, I am bankrupt without love.*

*1 Corinthians 13:1-7 Message Version*

# JOURNAL THROUGH

*Mr. And Mrs. Eric Cannon*

# OUR JOURNEY OF LOVE

# CHAPTER ONE

## The Call To Love

*Being confident of this very thing, he which hath begun a good work in you will perform it until the day of Jesus Christ. Philippians 1:6 (KJV)*

Loving God and people is the greatest commandment in *Matthew 22:37-40 (NIV)*, and it has always been God's intent. Therefore, I would further imply that God's vision for marriage goes beyond two people coming together, having children, being successful in careers, and whatever else we like to post on social media as relationship goals! God's original intent for marriage is to reflect his character and unconditional love for someone. Think about it?

Choosing to be bound with someone and consciously saying until death do us part is a huge commitment. Many people walk away from committed relationships because it seems easier to move on with another person than dealing with

17

issues within oneself. Even though we are in this world, we cannot be like this world, especially in loving ourselves and others. God's design for love, as mentioned in *1 Corinthians 13:4-8 (NIV), is Love is patient, Love is kind. It does not envy; it does not boast; it is not proud. It does not dishonor others; it is not self-seeking; it is not easily angered; it keeps no record of wrongs. Love does not delight in evil but rejoices with the truth. It always protects, always trusts, always hopes, always perseveres. Love never fails.*

We read this, but then life's difficulties alter our abilities, rendering it impossible to receive or present this love. My husband and I both have been previously married. Though I desired marriage again, I was scared. I'd been married twice, and my methods in those marriages were not of God. During the crash and burn of my second marriage, God revealed my destiny to me. We are all born with a purpose for our lives. God confirms our destiny in so many ways in His Word, and He continually shows me through dreams, confirmations of wise counsel, and prophetic messages that I not only was called to be a minister of the gospel but that my marriage would advance the kingdom of God as well. Once again, I had no clue how God would use a divorced woman to stand before people and talk about marriage. I am thankful to have trusted in my faith and see God as a redeemer and restorer. We may not understand why God calls us to do certain things or focus on specific areas, but we must be fully confident in knowing that God has a plan for us. What appeared as a failure was an opportunity in my life for God to do something unique. My faith in God was the invitation God needed to intervene. Before marriage, Eric was my best friend. I never thought he'd be my husband. We knew of one another flaws but wanted to be better for God before being anything to anyone else!

We were both guilty of doing marriage wrong, meaning we did it without the Holy Spirit. It was a desire for our ears to be so sensitive to Heaven that we'd hear the Holy Spirit fluently. The Holy Spirit awakened love within Eric, and he looked at me one day and asked could we become more than friends. I feared that moment because I knew if this was God's will, God was going to lead this thing his way. As we sought God on loving each other, we both experienced God heavily in our lives. God began pruning us and disturbing this flesh that was eager to sin. Our love for God and one another repeatedly brought us to a place of repentance. People testified of this heart transplant that happened within us. A transplant being symbolic of a transformation in God. We were committed to the process. We had begun to

> *Don't fear the moments of life, be assured that God will lead you into His will for your life.*

experience unconditional love before the marriage started, that we grew in love with each other based on God's vision.

The call on our lives became more massive than a wedding day. Our desires to please God became more significant than the desire to please self. God joined us together to embody the mantle of oneness. He chose us, two people with a past of three failed marriages, children out of wedlock, and abusive relationships from our past. The call to love is a call we answered to experience healing. Wholeness in God doesn't mean your marriage won't see days of growing pains. There will always be pruning and sharpening; however, God's love imparts assurance and security. This fulfilling love pours out of you then flows into the lives of others.

## Receiving The Love Of God

We were created to love God with all our minds, might, heart, and soul, then love our neighbor as ourselves. How do we do that? How do we surrender when the demands of life beckon for our attention? It begins with understanding who God is in your life. What do you need from God? I yearned for love from someone who would not judge me.

Is this you too?

If so, stroll through the foundations of love, marriage, and life decisions found within them.

I call these areas

- The Foundation
- The Frame
- The Crown (Rooftop)
- The Home God Built

In each section, you will see how God captured me from a state of despondency, wrapped my children within his glory, and intertwined my husband and I. God took the foundation of us, replaced it with himself, created the framework through life experiences, then covered us with His unfailing love. Our life decisions have a way of taking us down various paths only to end where it all began.

# The Foundation

## God and I

*The strength of a building lies within the foundation. This 1st dimension of Journaling Through Love represents the understructure of a home. A well-built foundation keeps others safe and is built to strengthen the structure of lives. Unfortunately, I was the home that didn't begin with a proper foundation. I had plans of perfection on top of God's plans for my life. It took God to realign and dismantle the life I created then build me on the foundation he created for me.*

*Let's Journal Through It…*

## CHAPTER TWO

### Past Perfections Brought Future Blemishes

*"Owe no one anything, except to love each other,
for the one who loves another has fulfilled the law."
Romans 13:8*

Since the beginning of my childhood, I have had a problem with perfectionism. It began with my parents and the expectations set upon me. Here is the thing, I knew how to perform. I knew how to put on a show for accolades. I knew how to look happy on the outside but miserable on the inside. I learned this from growing up in a household that I felt was like the Huxtable's to the world, but a grave mortuary of attempted happiness destroyed by my father's abusiveness to my mother. I remember I desired to be my mother's happiness, sticking close to her, and wanting her just to smile.

However, my father frequently used me to make my mother stay in a dysfunctional situation, and neither was right. My mother didn't ask me to become her crutch, but I became a perfectionist because of my helplessness to protect her. In the end, I was alone, feeling empty from the many cheerleading competitions to the games that I cheered at with no one in the stands. Numerous dance routines unseen, award days, with no one coming around the corners to bring me flowers. No one was there waiting with the other parents to say I'm proud of you. The disappointment list goes on and on. Since then, I have developed compassion for my mother and father to understand that they couldn't see past themselves. My parents couldn't give me the love they didn't have for themselves. So there lies the root if you haven't already figured it out. I learned love was something we earn. I then applied the same concept to my relationship with God! I thought I could be perfect, and God would grant all my wishes or that if I could be an ideal child, it would make my mom happy. However, you cannot achieve something that only God is and will forever be. I struggled daily with the concept of understanding how we cannot be "perfect" yet display perfect love.

> *I learned love was something we earn. I then applied the same concept to my relationship with God!*

My foundation was unstable. Little did I know that I had lessons ahead of me that would show me just how severe my perception of perfectionism would be. I was the foundation that weakened the structure leaving everyone vulnerable for attack. My college years exposed this side of myself.

I was attending college, dating the perfect boyfriend who loved me, so much so that he put up with all my crap and insecurities. I had at least 3-4 streams of income coming in from working for the college, a restaurant, a clothing store, and braiding hair. I was obsessed, and I freaked out when my bank account would hit under $500. I had a car and the best cell phone. I was homecoming queen in college, and the list goes on and on.

Stay with me; I'm getting to it!

I had it all, and together we had it all. I married my college sweetheart, but when he didn't add up to my perfect equation of what I thought marriage should be, I told him I wanted out and left him with no chance to reconcile. Don't forget I was a perfectionist, and that ruled my life.

I then met someone else who soon became my second husband. He was a chance at redemption to the "outside world" that I was married with kids, not just a single mother who got married. I managed to cover up what I didn't want others to see or know. I ran a tight ship that proved to be externally successful with many Facebook and Instagram vacation pics to show for it. I worked for the government, had the most prominent houses, 2 to 3 cars, and the best relationship the world could envision. Yep, I had built up the perfect life without God, although I went to church every Sunday and bible study on Wednesdays. I ministered in dance faithfully, but it wasn't until one Sunday I sat in my seat listening to the message. As the preacher was ending, everyone stood up, and as usual, the volume in the room got loud because people were shouting and crying out to God. Praise and Worship this Sunday was different. I had begun to feel as though I was losing my hearing. I could see the people praising God, but I could not hear anything. It was unreal!

Then my vision sharpened. My panic went away as I began to focus on specific people. I still felt as though I was better than those I saw worshipping God, yet; I was the one without feeling or emotion. I looked over at my husband, who was just starting with an indifferent disposition. My kids were asleep, but the other people…

The other people bothered me much because they seemed to be in a different place, much different from the happiness I created with this perfect life. They had joy and peace. One sister had her hands raised with this pure smile on her face; tears were streaming down from her eyes, and peace rested upon her. She lost her son to violence a little over a month ago. Where does she get that peace? I wondered. Another person was dealing with health issues, and she was jumping up and down, thanking God. I felt almost jealous because here I was, the one who had everything I ever wanted, but something was missing! I did not have what they had, and I wanted it. I needed it. We left services, but that memory lasted in my heart. The following Sunday, after I ministered unto God through dance, I ran to the altar asking God,

*When God is in your life. You have this joy and peace that is unexplainable. God himself radiates from you.*

> God, may I have the same relationship with you as these other people? God, I want a joy like that. May I have joy, peace, money, husband, vehicle, and the high rent house where we live?

God received my invite and came in. He began to correct all I attached his name to previously. We call them "God's blessings," even if they come from satan.

The rug of "comfortability" was pulled from under me slowly, day by day. It started when we became pregnant. I miscarried six weeks into the pregnancy, and guess how? Well, I decided to control the situation again by ministering in dance even though my husband expressed not to dance. Then the self-righteous woman I had become told him,

> "I've always been active with previous pregnancies. You can't tell me to stop praising God. I'll stop when I start showing."

On the way home, I remember feeling a cramp out of this world and looking at him like I need to get home. I went to the bathroom, and I was bleeding. We went to the hospital and waited so long in the waiting room that I passed the baby in the restroom. This situation was like a sword in my marriage. He rejected me and wouldn't give compassion, comfort, nor did he offer to hold my hand. How could I be so disobedient and not listen to him? I was shocked and disappointed in myself. His only response was, "I can't imagine how you could get pregnant so easily by men who didn't give a (you know what about me), yet you can't even hold a baby by me, your own husband." His response crushed me, left me breathless for a moment, and I believed him. What looked like heartache was God stripping me of this flesh that interfered with his purpose for me. About three months later, we found out that I was pregnant again! Now I know what you're thinking... Surely, I chose God now that He has blessed my womb again, right? Well, I didn't. I wanted the peace, but I didn't want to give up all that I'd obtained. I turned away from God altogether. I was pregnant with resentment. I resented God because I could no longer dance. I figured it's best to rely on ourselves because God's way required giving up too much. Time passed, and our time for having the baby was drawing near. He came sooner than expected because I was stressing about money. I wanted to make sure that I had enough money to continue our lifestyle because I knew I would be off work for at least three months with our baby. The sad part about it is, I only trusted what I could generate. During this, we had parents moving in and out. My nieces and nephews were coming to visit for the summer, and we were going through the motions.

There was this twinge of pain in my heart from being away from the church. The longer I stayed away from the presence of God (*The True Foundation*), the more I began to feel neglected by my husband. It seemed he thought if he worked that he didn't have to do anything else. I had to do everything else. He even asked, "Why do you need so much help? When you were a single mother, you did it all, so do it now." deep sigh. I was just there to play the casting role of super wife; his pride and joy was his son. This "perfect" life had me wanting to run away! I didn't understand why, though. Instead of running to the church, I ran into the arms of satan. Yes, it was the arms of another man. I was seeking validation, and I found it in another man.

Whew, that hurt just typing it. Even the wailing feeling of wanting to defend me wants to come through my fingers as I continue to type, but I admit that this is the truth, nothing but the truth, and it seems dark, but it gets better! I never had a physical relationship with the other gentleman, but I'd become emotionally detached from my husband. I needed someone else to validate how perfect I was, and although I genuinely desired the affection, attention, and approval from my husband, I gave myself an excuse. I told myself that it was okay for me to talk to that man because my husband wasn't giving me what I needed. As you know, talking led to extended lunch dates, finding excuses to go to the store by myself, to call him. I soon stopped caring about anyone else.

> Let God approve of you, give you the attention and affection you need. He makes our empty places "Full"

Until one day, I remember sitting across from this gentleman at one of our weekly lunch dates, and I burst out crying. Reality hit hard! I couldn't pretend or live a double life anymore.

My perfect little world was not so perfect!

Of course, Mr. Replacement did what any man would do and said what any man would say because he was patiently waiting for my marital status to change. He began to tell me how perfect I was, how my husband didn't deserve me, and so much more. He was feeding the little "perfection demon" within me and eventually kissed me after wiping my tears away! Now, if you were reading some love fantasy novel, you'd probably be like, "Yassssssss girl, you did that!" But NO! I jumped up, walked then ran as fast as I could to my car. When he jumped in front of me,

I said, "Don't ever contact me again. If I am going to lose my marriage, it won't be because of another man." I then decided to fight for the marriage! I began the 40-day Love Dare, and I sent my best friend an email confessing everything about the emotional affair I had with Mr. Replacement!

About two weeks later, just when my husband seemed to be breaking under the effects of the love dare, I walked into our home, and he's in front of my computer. He asked, "Asha, is there anything you want to tell me?"

My heart dropped! Correction, my heart sank literally... The marriage turned from a life of perfection into punishment from hell, where I experienced physical, mental, and verbal abuse! We started going back to church, but that was just a part of the abuse. My husband used the sermons as darts to condemn me, all while my husband did not want me to talk to anyone unless I was telling them how worthless I was and what I had done! Even from his pain, he wanted to see the perfect Asha suffer for being the perfect one in the relationship! He wanted people to know that *Mrs. Perfect Asha* wasn't so perfect. After the turmoil, I remember asking him would he ever love me again, and he said, "Maybe I will, maybe I won't, who knows."

I knew then that this punishment game would go on for some time unless we received counseling. We ended in divorce, and that decision shattered my entire world. I remember sitting in my niece's bedroom at my sister's house, thinking about how it got here. I just couldn't understand why God made me suffer like this!

I would love to tell you, God came down, sat on my bed, and told me everything would be alright. However, that's not what happened. Wouldn't you know that pride and perfection hang out together? I had to spiral out of control more!

In 2013, the divorce between my husband and I was granted. I thought once I divorced him, life would be great again, and my real Boaz would be waiting on me while I, like Ruth, was working hard in the fields! Honey, I became the worse overachiever you could imagine, and my Facebook page blew up because of excessive postings of trips, beautifully filtered pictures of me, and happy kids. I worked overtime and rented a house that showed I survived! Overall, I just wasn't getting it. I was still trying to prove a point! As long as I felt I was in control of my life, God was not!

In 2015 I was doing a side business of baking and working full time, taking care of my father in my house, and raising three kids. It wasn't as successful as it sounds! I was miserable! I was still without a husband and even considered online dating, which was a horrible bust.

I told you I would be real!

I needed God to interrupt my life, and he did. I started attending church again, becoming involved, and every message was hitting me in the heart once again. See, it is easy to blame others when your "perfect" plan isn't working. My ex-husband was to blame, my 1st child's father was to blame, my childhood was to blame, the fact that no one else in the world could deal with my perfection level was to blame. But then, there was no one.

> "God isolated me, and I hit a harsh reality that... I was the blame. No one else just me."

So, that Sunday evening, after the kids went to sleep, I went into my room and called *Mr. Commitment Issues*, a guy I wanted to marry, but his issues interfered. He came by to see me, and to my surprise, he only came over to tell me that he was choosing his ex over me and moving in with her. He had to cut off contact with me!

God didn't let me choose any other outlet but Him! Yet, I still tried something else. I had one more trick. I began to drink. My ex-husband had been calling, and this one time, he decided to come over, and what do you know, he found me on the floor listening to Drake. I was a hot mess. He stayed that night, and the next morning he made me get up and go to awards day for the kids. I could see the disappointment in his eyes. I then surrendered to God bit by bit. It was only His way that was going to work. I grew in faith and began believing visions that God showed me that motivated me to come out of the hole I dug myself in. Things were not perfect, but I was becoming okay with that.

Perfectionism is a hard thing to break because it requires you to have no control over the outcome, but that is the true essence of faith! God began to show me in His Word how much He loved me, how no mistake, nothing that I could do could ever separate us, and that all He wanted was a chance to right the wrongs, but I had to let go! Then I did. I finally let go. My ex-husband and I forgave each other. We accepted our faults and moved on.

## Journal This Moment

God doesn't want us to focus on performing perfectly; he wants us to focus on living out a childlike, dependent faith through authentic acts of love! The truth is my "perfect" love wasn't real! It was calculated! God's love began to rule out my calculations, and as I began to grow, he then introduced me to Eric. He and I invited God in, and God became our foundation.

# The Frame
## Jesus and I

During remodeling, the frame is being built, and the old walls and layers of false insulation must be torn down. The frame is the support structure built to hold up anything that sits on a stable foundation. This 2nd Dimension Of Journaling Through Love represents a frame that needed to be remodeled inside. God gave me someone who would help me receive His restoration. He used my marriage with Eric to reveal His heart of love for me and purify my heart. The framework is a part of God's process for my life and yours. God desired a home of friendship & marriage, where he could live and be our insulation.

*Let's Journal Through It...*

# CHAPTER THREE

## God Unmasked His Fears

*There is no fear in love. But perfect love drives out fear because fear has to do with punishment. The one who fears is not made perfect in love. 1 John 4:18 (NIV)*

This chapter will show how fear can become your identity. It can whisper lies in your head and attempt to distort God's perfect plan for His perfect love. Within these pages, you'll also notice how powerful love is within us, and when encompassed, we can emancipate not only ourselves but also others! Where do I begin?

Well, my husband, Eric, is a great place to start. It's incredible how someone's concerns can infiltrate your life, and it takes on the appearance of your own issues.

## Stolen Identity

When I met Eric, he had fears galore. Fear entered and stole his identity. There was the fear of long-distance traveling, fear of going over bridges, fear of choking, fear of eating in front of people, fear of death, fear of flying, fear of elevators, fear of people touching him on his shoulder, neck, or chest, fear of being in front of a church and near a large number of people (Imagine his tapping on chairs and leg shaking in the church to get through service).

On our first few dates, he created excuses for wanting us to eat and watch a movie at home. After a while, those excuses began dispersing into thin air. It was time to deal with the fears and overcome them. Many of his fears stemmed from childhood trauma and a few accidents but let's rewind, shall we,

Let's go back to the beginning and see how a husband and wife arrive at the destination of vulnerability among each other. It can be scary to show those sides to our partners out of fear of being judged, but this is how real intimacy is achieved. Eric gave me access to the areas of himself that had been deeply wounded.

How did he do that?

Well, we began as friends. I created a safe place in our friendship, a judgment-free zone for him to be himself. Now yes, of course, he knew that I was finer than wine (yep, I said it!), but he also knew that he couldn't approach me discussing a relationship status. My heart was fixated and centered on God's will for my life as a single mother of three kids, running a business and ministry. We began with a friendship. We were open with each other.

Eric told me things we needed to pray for, and I would pray earnestly for him because I knew in my heart that God was showing me his identity. My heart was heavy because of all the different labels of fear placed on him growing up. He'd been held back in life all because of a lack of true love. I felt as if no one prayed for him the way I did. The exciting moments of our friendship were our long conversations with one another. We believed in one another and experienced God's victory together over quite a few things that resulted from being honest and vulnerable.

> "Boy, this seems to be too much to dive into so soon in this book."

However, I'm going to continue. There were no expectations between Eric and me, just two people being real about our issues during that season. It was something about the way that we related to each other that made vulnerability safe. I remember the first time Eric asked me to date him; I looked at the phone like no way!

If there were a fist with, *get back in the friend zone written on it,* he would have felt it right on his forehead, laughing hysterically. Shortly after a few overnight conversations falling asleep on the phone and a couple of date nights, the words I love you hurried from our hearts and into each other. Eric said, "Asha, It is something about the way you believe in me that made me love you so fast; You love me the way I believe God loves me." Now, let me be completely transparent. On my end, I was saying I love you whenever Eric said it, but I had my reservations. I was fearful, but I soon came to terms with the fact that I had to let this man in my heart. I had introduced him to my children, we were together all the time, and God was telling me just to trust Him (not Eric but Him). The more I prayed to God, the more I actively loved Eric. I went all in, and although it was the rockiest

> *Create a safe environment that makes your partner say, you love me the way I believe God loves me.*

season of our relationship, Eric experienced healing! God began using our Love for one another to heal the fears within him. Sometimes healing comes in the darkest of times. Our relationships' darkest moments caused Eric's issues to be drawn out, and there were times he despised the process with me. We found out more in marriage how God has a way of bringing us face to face with ourselves.

On numerous occasions, Eric tried to break up with me, but I reminded him repeatedly that he wanted this relationship, and the times he tried were because of his unresolved fears! Being with me was like a truth serum that removed the lies he told himself about what love consisted of. God was exposing and casting out the tormenting fears through perfect love. The 1st to go was the fear of riding long distances. I was always traveling with my business and ministry. I also had to leave with my children for many weekends while he would stay home. Unfortunately, with all the issues we were having, he wouldn't allow me to keep traveling by myself, so that fear left.

The 1st time we rode to Atlanta, he burped, and we stopped a few times for him. I reached over and grabbed his hand. When I started laughing, making jokes, talking, and singing all of our favorite songs, his demeanor shifted. By the 2nd trip, he stared at me and squeezed my hand. Then the 3rd trip, he was wide open! He was staring out the window at the trees, the clouds, the different areas, and there were moments when his eyes were closed, yet he had a small smile on his face... That was freedom! He wanted to go all the time and was even ready to move from our hometown, which we did about seven months later! This step into the direction of freedom began to trickle in other areas of his life where fear had him bound. One day while we were in church, the words from the Bible came to life! He said, "Babe, I get it; I know love. I love you, and I know you love me!"

In his face was the most childlike excitement I had ever seen in a grown man! He explained how others pacified his fear and never pushed him to do something about it. No one ever prayed against fear or helped him to reject his worries. Even in my time of "studying" him, I would tell him things about himself, little triggers that I noticed before his anxiety would flare, which helped him pinpoint where the fear derived. This kind of assistance gave him the means to pull the root up and allow God to heal it! This also brings me to these points to ponder.

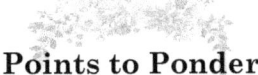
## Points to Ponder

1. How many times do we look at loved ones and say, I don't know what's wrong with that girl/boy without taking the time to love them through it?

2. How many times have we gone along with family, doctors, and friends' recommendations, assuming the behavior we see is our loved ones' real identity?

## *Journal This Moment*

Loving someone requires us to believe past what we see in the natural to what God says about a person. It is often easier to apply "unmerited" or unearned love to someone who is not as close as our family members. We must remember that loving others in a Godly way can bring forth healing.

## CHAPTER FOUR

### God Uncovered Her Scars

*He went to him and bound up his wounds,
pouring on oil and wine. Luke 10:34*

I shared a layer of my story in previous chapters, but this relationship revealed hidden fears as well. Fear hid within my wounds. I assumed I knew how to love and my "only issue" was no one knew how to love me. I'd convinced myself that I loved as God loves, but no one knew how to return that love to me, which left me feeling slighted. Even in the mentions above about my husband, I picked up a heart issue with God about why I needed to love him so hard even when he barely knew me. It didn't make sense, and I later realized that God's way for us to love one another doesn't make sense, but it yields results.

## A Blind Love

The scars of me wouldn't allow me to see with clarity. Everything seemed to be someone else's fault. Even in how Eric purchased gifts for me, I felt he was incapable of loving me accurately. I loved so hard in relationships before him yet always felt disappointed in people because of their inability to reciprocate love.

Then I'd make them feel horrible for how hard I loved them and their inability to measure up to the Godly love I deserved. I would read 1 Corinthians 13 and cry because I genuinely believed that it didn't apply to me to receive! I mastered the concept of giving it because I assumed this would bring love to me. God told me to look to him for love, but the truth is I wanted it in the form of a man first. I couldn't understand how I was such a good Christian but suffered so many failed relationships. Some guys would just break up with me and tell me that God said they weren't the one for me! Oh, how angry I became at God! In my relationship with Eric, I learned about myself and the need to be a strict ruler.

> Perfection is another way of saying I hate myself as I am. There's no way God could love me as I am, but He truly does.

This behavior was deep-rooted in fear masked as control. I was so controlling I withheld love from him and our children if they didn't act right, receive God right, or if I couldn't see that they were changing! I began to require things as if I were Jesus, and they had to show me changed behavior before they received whatever they were asking from God!

This is a true story!

I feel horrible writing this out, but there is freedom in truth, and more healing on my part found within my vulnerability with you! Eric helped open my eyes, and I can only imagine how my children felt before him. I saw my sweet mother, who was nearly an angel in my eyes, receive punishment from my father. I saw my brothers suffer from dysfunctional relationships, and one ended his life in suicide due to continuous unfortunate relational situations. I developed an uncanny sense of fear, and thus I felt the need to control. I hated how I grew up and the effects it had on my siblings and me. The very thing I created in myself to feel "accomplished" I was trying to put on my children.

One day, as I was going through deliverance (a spiritual experience of being set free from bondage), The minister said, "God's love is not a punishment." I read that very scripture in 1 John 4:18 KJV There is no fear in love two days prior. *But perfect love drives out fear because fear has to do with punishment. The one who fears is not made perfect in love.* The minister said, "Asha, you have a lot of fear!" I was thinking, no lady, I have a lot of hurts! The truth is, she was right! In a twisted way, I felt that to love God was to accept punishment because I would eventually die from love even in the early days of my life!

> *"Loving others meant, love them with no expectation of anything in return."*

So, I made "love" a transactional thing to protect me from fear. I thought that loving meant I had to become Jesus to people. I was wrong. Loving others meant to love them with no expectations of anything in return. I learned that my expectations should be on God. In thirty-eight years of living, this was the first time I felt an actual release of all the counterfeit love. I felt this overwhelming desire to love as God instructed. I immediately saw all the relationships surrounding me transform! I began to love without reciprocation because I wanted them to feel what God felt about me! When I released the fear of dysfunctional relationships, God was able to show me this unseen, unidentifiable huge truck of reckless love that slammed straight into my heart! That's the best way to explain it. This truck hit me and knocked off all the residue of conditional love, a love with transactions and terms.

God loves me so much that it was almost unbearable and overwhelming! I began to understand what it meant for God to chase you down to love you! When I started to see God's love, it caused me to see the love given to me, including my husband's gifts for me. The flowers now had a different meaning. He gave me flowers of all different kinds because I told him I hated roses. I remembered the ankle bracelet he gave me because he loved my small feet, and when I wore heels, how it adorned that part of me! I remembered all the times he cooked because I told him as a single mother, I used to be so tired from being a businesswoman and then putting on another hat as a chef, teacher to the kids, doctor when they were sick, etc. My husband's actions showed that this was God through him, his way of giving me the love I truly needed.

I began to love my children differently, and my ears could hear love. This behavior trickled down to my daughter. My daughter became so empowered by how I loved her that she stepped out and started her own business as a teenager! Not becoming a mini-me, her confidence in herself grew wildly because I wasn't there to cut it down when it didn't seem right to my standards. God had begun this great work where he dismantled walls that not only interfered in my life but our children's lives as well.

## *Journal This Moment*

*My deliverance caused an experience of God, which impacted my entire family. We all encountered God, and it was rewarding. We had no idea that God was building us all to strengthen our prayer life in him then. God was creating a stronger family bond with himself as the foundation and the frame. We were becoming the temple that God built. Who is going to be impacted by your deliverance? Who will you reach when you just let go and let God?*

## CHAPTER FIVE

## The Power Of Prayer

*Pray without ceasing and in everything give thanks for this is the will of God. 1 Thessalonians 5:17KJV*

When you pray, do you believe God will go abracadabra, and boom, things will change? Do you think that the very thing you are asking God to do in others, He will begin with you first? The power in praying is more than repetitive words to satisfy some obligation created. Prayer has the power to change everything, anything, and all things. Prayer is an intimate conversation between you and Almighty God. He cares so deeply for you and desires to be the answer to everything you need. We can be transparent with him because He becomes the protector, healer, and confidant willing to keep every secret, with no judgment. He is a parent that will wipe our tears. Prayer unto God is so beautiful. It involves speaking to God but also hearing God's voice. As you talk, he's attentive to every word.

He allows you to see a reflection of yourself within his truth. He unveils our eyes and changes our perspective. Usually, the areas we are praying about are areas where our viewpoint needs to be changed. I have often fallen to my knees in repentance because God simply held up the mirror (His Word). This truth in my life changed my perspective. Prayer is useful when it comes from the heart because what comes from the heart reaches the heart. It is so important to understand communication with God.

Prayer Changes:

- *You*
- *Immediate family*
- *Friend, enemies, and strangers*
- *It helps you to accept God's perfect will.*
- *It helps you to accept the perspective of others and still love with the love of God*

Journey with me as I give some of my most transparent moments in comprehending the power of prayer and how

Childlike prayer healed our family. I have always prayed for God's perspective of relationships and marriages for my children. I did not want my mistakes and failures from previous marriages to affect them. I'd say, God, I want my children to have productive relationships and fruitful marriages despite what they have seen. My condemnation led me to this prayer that caused me to choke and limit God. Alas, after going more in-depth in worship, God revealed how he'd take care of them.

> "The Prayers of the righteous man are both powerful and effective."

What God revealed to me about myself ironically has helped me love them better and consider their perspective on how they needed to be loved! This kind of teaching from God to my children has helped them learn and understand how to be loved. God is using this marriage now as a teaching tool for our children. It's as if God allowed them to see my failures to learn how to make better choices.

The marriage between Eric and I consist of eight kids. Three are mine, and four are his from a previous marriage with one from a prior relationship.

Need more clarity?

Sure, I'll break it down even more; my children have three different fathers within our blended family. The relationship between myself and my oldest daughter's father was short-lived. He and I were never married. My middle son is from another relationship, which he and I never married. My youngest son is from my ex-husband. As for my husband, he had a child with a woman in which they never married. Then he had four children with his ex-wife. This gives us a total of *FIVE* perspectives on how to raise children, *FIVE* different households to consider, and FIVE other additional adults who may or may not even consider God as their source!

## My Beautifully Blended Family

When it came time for my husband and me to blend our families, it was a breeze on my end. My husband loves my children as his own, and my children's fathers wanted to make sure there would be an excellent male role model present. However, for his children and previous partners, the blending process took more time. We had to deal with not seeing the children because of issues with the mother. My husband cried many nights because all he wanted to do was be a good father. You see, my husband lost his father at the age of two and did not remember him. Although his mother remarried, Eric's relationship with his stepfather wasn't the best. He wanted to give his children what he didn't have. This is where the burning prayer for our children began. Our prayer was simple.

### Blended Family Prayer

*Lord help us to have a consistent relationship with Eric's children. Remove any hindrances that are keeping Eric from being part of his children's life. Forgive us for not being the best parent or handling things according to the standard you have set concerning the gift of children you gave us despite the divorce. Help our exes to forgive us as we extend forgiveness to them. Touch the heart of our exes, that each one will consider the best interest of the children. Help us to have the best interest of the children as well.*

Honestly, it appeared the more we prayed; it seemed that the opposite was happening. At one point, Eric's ex wouldn't allow communication with us, and her family kept saying that she didn't have a phone.

After about a week of no calls or contact, we decided to find a lawyer, and then before we made contact, we received a phone call from his ex-wife. She revealed that she needed the kids to come and live with us because she did not have her own place. Little did we know that the department of family and children were contacted regarding this matter and other concerns involving the children. We had been praying that same prayer for only a week before this phone call! God moved quickly! Unfortunately, this did not happen without a small fight because she wanted to put stipulations on how we were to get the children and everything just to be petty, but we began to pray harder! After two days of going back and forth, finally, the caseworker advised her and us that if the children did not come and live with us, they would be placed in foster care. When we met, I remember feeling sorry for her. I knew the position of being a mother and feeling like you were losing the one thing that made you feel loved, your children. I encouraged her to use this time to get herself together. Every woman, including myself, needs the necessary time to heal so we can be better mothers. I understood. At that moment, God told me to

> *Every woman, including myself, needs the necessary time to heal so we can be better mothers.*

apologize to her, and without hesitation, I did! I apologized for whatever she had endured, even from my husband! I felt compassion take over me as if I was looking at myself! Something broke, and we both shed some tears. I knew that God was doing something bigger! I still pray for their mother. We do have moments of indifferences as she despises the fact that the kids call me mom, but I know that she will be okay. I pray for her to heal.

I can genuinely say that his children receive an overdose of love not just from us but from our church family, my family, and our close friends. They have experienced something that we ALL longed for, and that is.... stability! From my husband's perspective, being a "stepchild," we have the rule that there is no such thing as "step" in our house!

I know the love that my husband has for his children. I love them just as hard as my own, and quite honestly, they not only need it but also deserve it. I must give a tremendous amount of respect to my children as well for sharing me. Sure, they had moments where they felt like I was being pulled from them, but I continually ask God to nudge me if, at any point, my children needed me just a little bit more! It has been a balance that has turned out beautifully. Many dysfunctional situations on both ends have changed not because of anything we did ourselves but honestly because of prayer's power!

I have forgiven myself for getting pregnant before marriage. I have raised my children to know the love of God and teaching them that prayer changes things, and God has stood firm in never letting those prayers go unanswered. I will bring this point home to show you how prayer has helped heal areas concerning the children, some of the other parents, and how we co-parent! The kids always prayed for their other parents, and to hear them pray for their fathers made me realize that I had to pray for them also. When I would give them the chance to pray every night, I was always amazed at the trust and faith they each had in God despite what seemed to me to be a broken situation. They trusted that God heard their prayers, and they knew all parents loved them. The prayers also kept them from being separated from each other. Sometimes they would even say, "Can we call our dads to pray with them too?"

Imagine me, trying to be all hurt and bitter after that! They believed precisely what we taught them about the power of prayer! Over the years, co-parenting has been a blessing! One of my son's fathers got married, and his wife loves my son just as much as I do! My oldest daughter's father began to come around more, and they spend time with each other consistently! Our kids' prayers were more substantial than all the hurts, bad breakups, and emotional divorce! As parents, we all are living out their prayers. Even others who witness it ask how is it that y'all get along so well without all the drama? They say it's these crazy kids; I say it's their "crazy" prayers! Now don't get me wrong, there are times where there are slight disagreements, and due to uncertainties in their lives, it does affect ours. However, we have learned to take everything to God in prayer still, and we see time and time God works it out! My children have healthy relationships with all their fathers. I have a husband who loves our children, and through the power of prayer, my husband has forgiven himself and his ex. The children don't have to grow up thinking when our parents got divorced; our father divorced us too. Our family is evidence of God's redemptive power. The power of prayer has transformed our "statistics." The power of prayer has taught us that sometimes the things we can't fix in others, even the situations we created out of our disobedience, can be transformed by the power of love and compassion.

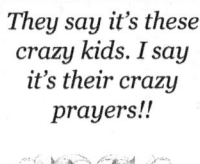

*They say it's these crazy kids. I say it's their crazy prayers!!*

We pray for each person connected to us because, like it or not, our children's' lives are affected by their existence. Learning to love even when met with opposition can be difficult, but when you see the reward of praying for those that have hurt you and loving them. It's such a fantastic experience that neither Eric nor I can take the credit. It is nothing but the love of God that can heal in this way. What was once an ugly situation for the both of us has turned into something beautiful. I would have never imagined it would have turned out this way! I encourage you at this moment to try praying without ceasing until you see God transform those relationships in your life that may be difficult. We have experienced transformation through prayer that will destroy generational curses in dysfunctional homes, divorce, and rejection.

*We are proof that prayer indeed changes things*

## *Journal This Moment*

*I encourage you that if you have a blended family, pray for the other parents as you pray for your children's well-being. Look at them and want your children to be proud to call them mom or dad. Ask God to heal the hurts that cause the strife between you all for the sake of the children, and trust that He will do it! Remember, this is bigger than you. Yes, your feelings matter; we want you to view the complete picture.*

## CHAPTER SIX

### I Can't Bake This Up

*When the righteous cry for help, the LORD hears and delivers them out of all their troubles. Psalm 34:27 NKJV*

Healing and deliverance can happen in stages, or it can happen instantly. God revealed areas of my heart, where I buried the perfectionism. It hid within the business. I found healing during this journey of building my side business, and that was the last bit of control I released from my job! I worked for the government, and the benefits were excellent. While I didn't care for what I did, I was good at it even though I was always stressed! I experienced one crisis after another at this job. My father was sick, and I lost my brother. I became ill and eventually accepted that I heard God correctly when He said to leave my job! Now, I won't get into the fullness of details around me, leaving my job to start a baking business, but God created the opportunity for me.

I can't bake that up (pun intended on the name of my next book coming out, "I can't bake this up!" He used the most unlikely skill that I didn't go to school to complete numerous things within me at once, such as to lead me, give me the courage to heal, leave my job, and develop an incredible relationship with my children. I've had to depend solely on God regarding my skills of baking and decorating amazing cakes. This business brought me home to open my first storefront location, minister to those who knew who I was in the past, and for others to meet my husband, Eric!!! I would love to tell you that I am completely healed from being a perfectionist, but it has been a conscious work. People will come and go when you have a ministry. There is no such thing as living the perfectly isolated "booed up" life with your hubby and kiddos! In this beautiful freedom that I am experiencing, walls are falling. I am laying aside every weight and placing them at his feet. Jesus already died on the cross for our sins, so I don't have to be in control and have the final say in a person's life.

> God will call you to do something that your education can't take the credit for.

My love and compassion for ministry outweigh my frustration of perfected endings being bought into fruition by my hands. The desire I once had to feel validated by my works has weakened, and the only thing that validates anything in my life at this point is to be perfectly IMPERFECT!

In my imperfection, I realize I can never measure up to Jesus; that's a lot of leveling up!!! God gives the Bible that provides us with many examples of people, that accepted the call to be used with fear and trembling. These people simply believed in Jesus Christ, and they became perfect miracles in the lives of others who witnessed! Do you notice my usage of the word perfect throughout this chapter? It is intentional because I continuously struggled with this word and the identity of perfection.

I now know there is no charge for Godly love, but the benefits of pursuing love and pursuing trusting God with all our hearts become full of advantages that nothing we can do so perfectly will ever measure up to the salvation we receive when we become His. I have regained more than I lost when I let go. Even this chapter alone is a true testament that God in my life. *Revelation 12:11 KJV has become true in my life, which says, and they overcame him by the blood of the Lamb, and by the word of their testimony; and they loved not their lives unto the death.*

## Journal This Moment

The ultimate sacrifice of Jesus dying on the cross and the truth of the power of His saving grace through my testimony made me detest the life of control. I can't bake this up is just that, and you have to decide that you can't bake this up or makeup areas of your own life that would seem perfect. This pattern is control and lack of trust in God. I assure you the more you fall in love with God. You, too, will fall in love with yourself.

# The Crown

## The Holy Spirit and I

*The purpose of the rooftop is to offer protection from any outside elements that attempt to infiltrate. This 3rd Dimension of Journaling through Love represents God's seals upon us. He is our covering, and he teaches us how to cover one another. He became our life, love, marriage, ministry, and it's out of his teachings and everlasting love towards us that we are growing into who we are today.*

*Let's Journal Through It...*

# CHAPTER SEVEN

## You can only play one position

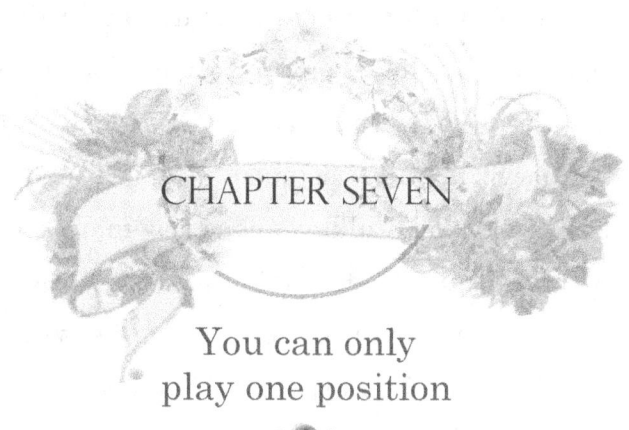

*Stand firm, hold your position,
and see the salvation of the LORD on your behalf, 2Chronicles 20:17 ESV*

In marriage, a husband is like a quarterback. The husband is the leader of the household, as the quarterback is the leader on the field. A quarterback's position is to see an opening and communicate with the other players to get them to an opening! He also sees where there is danger and won't put the other players in a position to get tackled or give up the ball to be intercepted. He's the one with all the plays memorized in his head and can choose which ones work best given the opponents and how they play! The quarterback teammates must trust that he sees the bigger picture from his perspective on the field. My husband broke this down to me one day in his many rambling sessions, and I was like, "Why are we talking about football and not our marriage!" I thought it was one of his ploys to get out of having a long drawn out emotional discussion with me as I like to drag him through ever so often. Still, once I listened to him, it made all the sense because we were talking about how many marriages we know of (not just traditional marriages but Christian marriages) where they are married yet the wife doesn't trust the husband or vice versa, so they have a relationship where they are doing their own thing! When it comes to finances, some have separate hidden accounts. One or both keep lock codes on their phones so the other won't be privy to specific conversations. Some have more than one Facebook page that shows family and the other as if they are almost single! There is an aspect that says I want to be married, but I have a backup plan if this doesn't work out.

> *The husband, just like the quarter back must see danger ahead from the opponent and provide safety for the family.*

There is also the concept of the one in the marriage that does everything because they don't trust that the other will do anything right. None of these concepts genuinely represent God's vision for a Godly marriage, yet we see it often displayed in Christian marriages!

I, too, had to learn from my husband's example through football that at one point, I didn't trust him to be the man of the household. I was just letting him wear the title. How many times do we keep asking a person repeatedly to be something then take the opportunity from them to become it? Sometimes we forget we had to learn and be allowed to make mistakes to become better!

I decided to put love and trust in this chapter because you can only love something you know. You only trust something that you know. The word love is the most abused and misused term. Through marriage, I've learned that the more you love someone, the more it becomes a growth tool, but when we want to control situations, circumstances, outcomes, and so forth, resentment arrives within the heart.

### Ways resentment settles within our lives

- Resentment can come when someone isn't doing it the way you want it done instead of loving the fact that someone wants to learn or desire to do whatever "it" is!
- Resentment comes when we are tired, yet when someone asks you to help, you say you got it because you don't trust that it will get done.

- Resentment comes when one spouse refuses to be vulnerable. All while that is the purpose of love.
- Resentment can't settle in our hearts and remain there when we understand love's purpose. The purpose of love is to transform us, so we trust and open our hearts to God and each other!

Then I had a light bulb go off; many people confess to loving God but don't know Him! They claim to know Him, but when it's time to trust Him, they would rather pretend in the role of him attempting to become a savior to others, hence playing all positions! Can you imagine a one-person football team? It sounds ridiculous, right? But there are people out here playing "family" while everyone else is riding the bench! There are many Christians in the world proclaiming to love Jesus, but when asked to turn from riches and follow Him, they walk away.

*"Without Trust in God There's no Power in Position"*

These false saints continue in their rituals of bible study, Sunday services, and church gatherings rather than live a life that requires total dependence and faith in following God's ordered steps.

## Trusting God, No Matter What

Trust and love are two words of action! Trust is when you firmly believe in the character, strength, or truth of someone or something. When you believe in truth, there is a knowing which brings forth security. This knowing is called discernment. Many choose partners with no wisdom or pure truth within them. These false relationships show a sad reality of insufficient trust with highly celebrated platforms, which clarifies *Matthew 9:37 NKJV. Then He said to his disciples, The harvest is plentiful, but the workers are few.*

Many of our friendships, relationships, and family members need to experience God through our behavior and love toward them because we are representatives of Christ. If trust is damaged among close connections and you've begun labeling yourself as an introvert due to your hurts, then observe your relationship with God. It is crucial to examine your heart and trust in God! Read the Bible and focus on the word trust in various scriptures. Observe the usage of the word and apply it to your life. *Psalm 118:8-9 NLT says It is better to take refuge in the Lord than to put confidence in mortals. It is better to take refuge in the Lord than to put confidence in princes.*

If you have hurt one another, please let's repent and ask for forgiveness. It is hard to trust those who have hurt us, and it's even harder to trust God when your view of Him has been tainted due to the behaviors of others. We trust in the wrong things, and when what we have placed our trust in fails us, then we blame God!

Ironic right?

The fact is we have failed at this since the beginning of time. However, this Christian walk has always been about us experiencing Christ's salvation, grace, forgiveness, unconditional love, and releasing Him into the lives of others.

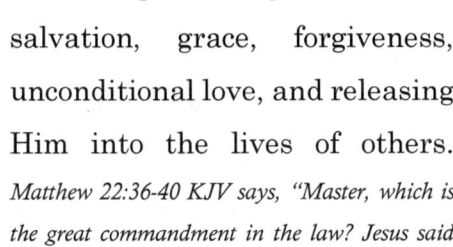

*Love one another as unto God for the rest of your life without seeking an escape plan even when things don't go as you planned.*

Matthew 22:36-40 KJV says, "Master, which is the great commandment in the law? Jesus said unto him, Thou shalt love the Lord thy God with all thy heart, and with all thy soul, and with all thy mind. This is the first and great commandment. And the second is like unto it; Thou shalt love thy neighbor as thyself. On these two commandments hang all the law and the prophets." He breaks it down in this very scripture how our love first for Him, with all our hearts, helps us to love others as we love ourselves, which requires little do with Him telling us to trust the other persons but simply just to love! My marriage has taught me to do this effectively is to be a bondservant of Christ committed to loving as Christ. Loving someone for the rest of my life with the understanding and knowing that an escape plan can't be implemented. We both must seek God and trust God together. The football analogy my husband gave me at the beginning of this chapter can easily be used when thinking about your relationship with Christ and your church.

## Self-Examination Questions

1. How many of you can say you know the vision of your pastor?
2. What is your position on the team?
3. Do you play a part on the team to help the vision come to pass?
4. Are you attending church for your comfort without gaining more souls for Christ?
5. Do you realize that the ultimate goal is for you to help draw others to Christ?

## *Journal This Moment*

*Take this chapter and think of how loving and trust go hand in hand. Begin to analyze what or who you give your love to, as well as who you trust. If the belief and connection outweigh your "love" for God, then make the necessary adjustments to know that God would never put you in a situation where your trust for another will outweigh His love, direction, and concern for your life! It takes loving God **100%** and continuously working to know Him through His word that will help you, love, forgive, care for, teach, and so much more, all who Christ died on the cross to save.*

# The Home God Built

## God, Jesus, Holy Spirit and I

*The final stage of your home is in the presence of God. This is where your heart is, and your heart should be in God. I am, and you are the home that God built. This 4th Dimension of Journaling through Love is a representation of God choosing to place his spirit within us. He has reconstructed my life all for the sake of love, and I didn't have to be perfect to be loved. He just desires to dwell within you and me. Will you accept his invitation to take you on a journey as he inscribes his love, trust, and peace into your heart? Christ said, Behold, I am with you always, even to the end of the age." Matthew 28:20 NIV*

*Let's Journal Through It…*

# CHAPTER EIGHT

## Love Isn't Enough

*Let love be without hypocrisy. Abhor what is evil; cling to what is good. Romans 12:9 NASB*

I am writing about a love story, but for me to end by saying love isn't enough, let me explain! You know I won't leave you hanging; After all, I've shared my heart with you, in the name of love! There are nights when I can't sleep, and I question everything. I think that there will never be such a thing as perfection, yet there is this never-ending strive for it. There is no one perfect, no not one, other than The One that walked the earth blameless for my sins, was bruised, scarred, and died a horrible death just so that I can be free. It hurts to celebrate it, knowing I will never reach the potential to be so deserving of such a swap. Every day, I wake up by the grace of God, dying an intentional death by the power of God. I ask for forgiveness because I deem myself unworthy. I only hope to believe that by the power of God within me, I can represent Him to someone else who is an unbeliever.

I don't believe in fate or by chance because no one can orchestrate as He can. I choose to believe in Jesus Christ because it is impossible for anyone to love me as He does. Nobody can come through for me as He has. Even in the most tragic moments, I look back to see the divine purpose of God. There are so many instances that I can tell you of how He came through for me, but instead, you think back to the last time God protected you. Think about the time where you said, "God if you just free me from this, I'll never do that again." Only to do it again, and realize He loves you, still! Think about how He made a way literally out of no way at the last hour! This is God's character, and it is because of His love for us all. God has a plan for our lives that no matter how badly we mess up, he's there. *Romans 8:39 NLT. Who will separate us from the love of Christ? Will hardship, or distress, or persecution, or famine, or nakedness, or peril, or sword? As it is written, "For your sake, we are being killed all day long; we are accounted as sheep to be slaughtered. No, in all these things, we are more than conquerors through him who loved us. For I am convinced*

> *Even in the tragic moments of life. God is there building a pathway of blessings leading directly to Him.*

*that neither death, nor life, nor angels, nor rulers, nor things present, nor things to come, nor powers, 39 nor height, nor depth, nor anything else in all creation, will be able to separate us from the love of God in Christ Jesus our Lord."*

My husband and I have lived a life that proves God has no limitations in how he loves. We decided to marry in God and for his purpose. Here I am with a husband who loves God more than he loves me. My husband's love and commitment are a resemblance to Godly love! God used someone I placed in the "friend zone" for nearly nine months, yet he was someone that I prayed with, shared all my secrets with, vented to about the guys that I thought I was interested in, and laughed with about the corniest of things and so forth. I was the girl that didn't judge him, never expected anything out of him, but for him to grow into everything he told me God said He would be. I believed in his dreams and visions and wasn't afraid to ask him to stop downplaying God's call on his life. I prayed in previous months for my husband before I knew the identity of my

> *I believed in him and wasn't afraid to say,*
> *" Stop downplaying God's call on your life. "*

husband. He was right there all along. In that season, my dear readers, I did NOT love Eric. What I had for him was a healthy friendship, free of expectation, and full of patience. I was just thankful to have someone who let me be me...authentically, flawed, and full of love for God that both gave us hope for better days ahead! Eric was unselfish with me even though his experience with females consisted of selfishness. Only the brotherly love (Agape Love) made him desire more from me even though he hadn't known what I was like sexually. There was a spark in our conversation that would have us on the phone for hours talking about God, our dreams, our plans, and I began to listen and intercede for him like I never did for anyone else.

Imagine all this happening

without us saying I love you!

Well, it was during our friendship that this occurred! I learned through our friendship what *2 Peter 1:5-7 meant. For this very reason, applying your diligence [to the divine promises, make every effort] in [exercising] your faith to, develop moral excellence, and in moral excellence, knowledge {insight, understanding}, and in your knowledge, self-control, and in your self-control, steadfastness, and in your steadfastness, godliness, and in your godliness, brotherly affection, and in your brotherly affection, [develop Christian] love [that is, learn to seek the best for others unselfishly and to do things for their benefit].* I am sad to say, yet grateful to have experienced the true meaning of loving someone who prepared me for what the ministry of marriage is all about. Godly love transforms someone into a person you could've never fathomed you would expect. If

I told you of my husband and me, who we use to be, and what we used to participate in, you would say BUT GOD! We both have experienced harmful and hurtful deeds in the "name of love." We still choose every day to live a life based on what we believe within our living word-the BIBLE, and it is the best love we've ever had! Marriage has been a fulfilling faith journey because it truly represents Christ's relationship with His bride (the church).

## What Are A Few Responsibilities Within Marriage?

- Marriage is a physical view of God's supernatural covenant with us chosen for each of us from the very beginning.
- It's the responsibility of a man to choose to lead while understanding how to be led by Christ and be the greatest servant.
- It is the wife's responsibility to care for and be submissive to her leadership while raising others to love, nurture them back to health and submit to a vision bigger than she knows!
- In the confines of marriage, it shows the world how two people can choose to listen before speaking,

solve problems, not just block or delete a person out of your life (which is so easy to adapt to in this day and age per social media)
- Remain committed to God when someone isn't your ideal person at all times.

This ministry isn't to be taken as light-heartedly as many do without truly understanding how to love as Christ loves. It's a blessing because you learn how to persevere, stand for something other than yourself, fall in love over and over again, and most importantly, trust in God who says in *Ecclesiastes 4:9-12 (NIV) Two are better than one because they have a good return for their labor: If either of them falls, one can help the other up. But pity anyone who falls and has no one to help them up. 11 Also, if two lies down together, they will keep warm. But how can one keep warm alone? 12 Though one may be overpowered, two can defend themselves. A cord of three strands is not quickly broken.*

Please understand that whoever you marry, they are human and will still have their moments. This time I'm going the distance, and I have to be willing to accept the bad parts of Eric along with the good!

*"This Battle Belongs to God."*

We work on being best friends every day, and anything that we can't handle, we simply say, "This battle belongs to God."

We make a conscious effort not to fight with each other but join hands to fight an enemy that hates what he forfeited to have! There are moments where he has prayed for me for our family, with tears rolling down his face. He has held me during my deepest fears. I tell him I love him despite the downright embarrassing moments that God places on his heart to say to me about his past. We still cry and pray through it while thanking God for change. When our kids see the healthiest version of love in our marriage, it becomes worth it, and then it becomes ministry. I've never been given this much grace from other guys, and he's never received this much forgiveness and belief in himself from other females. We've never received so many prophetic words and confirmations about our union. God has never discarded us, and we will not discard each other. Why do we have this mentality regarding marriage? Well, we made a vow that we want to love; and we want God! If you are single, I encourage you to desire God more than you want

> *We made a vow that we want love; and above all we just want God!*

anything else: whether it's a career, marriage, a designer purse, or a strong Starbucks caramel macchiato with an extra shot of espresso (I'm telling on myself here, laughing) but just want more of Him! He's the only one that created you, and He knows what's best for you.

## *Journal This Moment*

*If you're married, I recommend desiring God more than you desire anything else, more than you want your husband to be more like your "dream husband," more than the house, the babies, and more than the perfect life you desire. There's no life without God, and you can't treat your spouse the way they deserve to be treated without the heart of God! (I remind myself all the time that even when Eric and I are in heated fellowship, he too is a child of God.*

## CHAPTER NINE

### Love the Hell Out Of Them

*Whosoever calls on the name
of the Lord shall be saved. Romans 10:13 KJV*

Remember, anything you do for love will never be about you but for the next person's betterment. We have that much power that you can love the "hell" out of someone literally if you love them the right way...the Godly way. We can transform atmospheres through our application of the Word of God. The power we possess comes from the Holy Spirit, and through this love, we can save someone from going down the wrong path. God's love says, "You're worth more!" Our version of love has attachments, demands, conditions, and dysfunctional behavioral patterns from previous situations. When God, who is love, lives within you, we love the way He requires. Love conquers all and covers a multitude of sins. God sent His only begotten son to die for everyone in this world so that they may have the freedom and accept the beautiful gift of salvation. Many times, on my journey and still until this day, I remind myself, Romans 10:13 says, Whosoever calls on the name of the Lord shall be saved.

> "God is not mad at us nor is he holding us hostage in the sin. He loves us and is here to help."

The term, whosoever, means you!

You may hear people ask, are you saved? There may be some that ask about your salvation in God. How do you know whether you will live with Jesus Christ for all of eternity? Have you received the Holy Spirit? Salvation means saving human beings (souls) from death (Hell) to Eternal Life in Christ. There is no separation from God because of Christ's death, burial, and resurrection. We can enjoy an intimate relationship with God here on earth and in Heaven.

If you have not accepted Christ as your savior and you would like to fall in love with Our wonderful God, then repeat these words,

## Prayer of Acceptance

Dear God,

*I want to be a part of your family. You said in Your Word that if I acknowledged that You raised Jesus from the dead and accept Him as my Lord and Savior, I would be saved.*

*So, God, I believe You raised Jesus from the dead and that He is alive and seated in Heavenly places. I accept Him now as my personal Lord and Savior. Lord, I need you.*

*I accept my salvation from sin right now.*

*Jesus is my Lord and Savior.*
*Thank you, Father God, for forgiveness, salvation, and eternal life with you. Amen!*

## Welcome to The Family

Congratulations_____,
(Insert Name)

What now?

- Get involved in a local Bible-based church!
- Learn about who God created you to be.
- Let God love you. Yes, all of you, even the bad parts.
- Discover Your Purpose in Life!

Family is waiting for you in the body of Christ. We are ready to serve you and be served with your gifts and talents!!

Love you, brother/sister!

# CONCLUSION

It is indeed my prayer that by now, you have learned the love that I speak of is the most potent transforming and internally changing love from God! It is through being loved correctly from the only power source of love that I have indeed been able to love others how He has commanded! I pray that you look at each situation in your life that you are currently going through and move forward with an understanding of what is real love, what and who needs more love, and what is false love. Then apply the Word of God to not only yourself but the standard of which others are held in your heart. Although this love story doesn't encompass all the issues of life, I am confident that if you apply God's Word to any situation concerning love, how to be loved, and how to love, it all starts with the creator of love.

When it comes to raising children, God's love wiped away my guilt, shame, and condemnation and showed me that because I am blessed and reconciled with Him, so are my children. The love of God helps me defeat generational curses for my children.

When it comes to being a divorcee and being fortunate enough to experience remarriage, God's love gave me forgiveness! God showed me in His word that although divorce is something He hates, under no circumstance does He allow others to condemn or denounce what He did not put together. Through deep studying of His Word, I found healing in understanding that the reason God hates divorce (not me) is because of what it does to the children, each person involved, and the faith of those who may have come to believe in love through the union of marriage.

God, has shown me the power of redemption, forgiveness, and restoration to keep His promises despite my mistakes! Lastly, God's love has given me a deep sense of understanding of real repentance. It is more than just being sorry. Repentance is a conviction of remorse and sincere regret. The convictions are so strong that you do not want to hurt God by committing the same sin willingly. When you are madly in love with someone, it changes how you see and deal with everything and everyone! If you've ever loved someone so deeply, you would never want to intentionally nor unintentionally do anything to mess up that relationship.

What makes repentance real is when you realize you have messed up, and then God still blesses you, puts you in a position to advance you, loves you to provide for you, and, most importantly, when He forgives, He FORGIVES! It's His relentless love that makes you turn from anything that's not like Him or that would come in between your relationship with him! So, as I end this book, I pray that it is a beginning for you! A start or further advancement in trying to wrap your mind around the radical, unconditional, overwhelming love of God and then apply it to not only yourself but your spouse, neighbors, children, family, co-workers, church laborers, and anyone else that crosses your path.

*I pray that love transforms your life, and your relationships and excellent fruit come from it! Truly, God's love is indeed what we are created for, and whether you know it or not, it's what we crave!*

# Living Water Books Missions Statement

*You trust your God-given vision in our hands, and it is our mission to connect, embrace, build, and breathe life into the writings that record all that God has allowed, inspired, and led you through. Your life is a story to be shared.*

*We spread the word of God from his heart through your hands and out into the world. God's living waters flowing through writings will cause lives to flourish and transform hearts with truth.*

# THE PUBLISHER

## Living Water Books is The Christian Imprint of Butterfly Typeface Publishing

*He who believes in me from his Innermost being Will flow continuously, Rivers of Living Water.*

*John 7:38*

Website: https://livingwaterbooks.org/

Contact Us for All Your Publishing, Graphics and Designs.

470-344-3891

www.ingramcontent.com/pod-product-compliance
Lightning Source LLC
Chambersburg PA
CBHW070940080526
44589CB00013B/1590